120

QUOTATIONS EVERY EDUCATED PERSON SHOULD KNOW

Compilation and Commentary
By
Lawrence Newman

120 Quotations Every Education Person Should Know

TO THE READER

Over the years I took up the habit of collecting quotes that I found inspiring, humorous, informative, and historically enlightening. Many of these quotes are contained within the pages that follow.

I don't always agree with the quotes but didn't feel my own feelings should be the basis for exclusion of a thought provoking statement.

In several cases I've included my own comments about the quote, sometimes based on my understanding that developed over time, and sometimes to give the reader the historical context.

I hope you enjoy this collection of quotes I've selected, which I believe every educated person should know.

L. Newman
February 5, 2016

120 QUOTATIONS EVERY EDUCATED PERSON SHOULD KNOW

"I am become Death, Shatterer of Worlds."—Robert J. Oppenheimer, leading scientist of the Manhattan project, which developed the atomic bomb, remembering the line from the Indian scripture *Bhagavadgita*, after witnessing the world's first nuclear explosion in the early morning darkness of July 16, 1945 in the desert of New Mexico.

"A lie can travel half way around the world before truth gets its boots on."—Mark Twain

"In vino, veritas." (In wine, there is truth)—Pliny the Elder (Be careful what you say "under the influence").

"Two roads diverged in a wood, and I took the one less traveled by. And that made all the difference."—Robert Frost from his poem "The Road Not Taken".

"Victory has a hundred fathers but defeat is an orphan."—Galeazzo Ciano

"Political power grows out of a barrel of a gun."—Mao Tse-Tung

"One definition of insanity: Doing the same thing over and over again expecting a different result"—Albert Einstein

"No good deed goes unpunished."—Brooks Thomas

"Abandon all hope, ye who enter here!"—From Dante's *Divine Comedy--The Inferno*

"Give a man a fish and you feed him for a day. Teach him to fish and you feed him for a lifetime."—Chinese proverb

"You can't go home again."—Author Thomas Wolfe, used in the sense that you can't return to a time of your earlier life and have the same experience—people and places change.

"Well, I don't know as I want a lawyer to tell me what I cannot do. I hire him to tell me how to do what I want to do."—J. P. Morgan

"All animals are equal, but some animals are more equal than others." —Restatement of the farm animals' original "commandments" by the pigs after they had consolidated their control of the farm—from George Orwell's *Animal Farm*.

"In Germany, they came first for the Communists, and I didn't speak up because I wasn't a Communist. Then they came for the Jews, and I didn't speak up because I wasn't a Jew. Then they came for the trade unionists, and I didn't speak up because I wasn't a trade unionist. Then they came for the Catholics, and I didn't speak up because I was a Protestant. Then they came for me, and by that time no one was left to speak up."—Attributed to Martin Niemoeller

"I went to the woods because I wished to live deliberately, to front only the essential facts of life, and see if I could not learn what it had to teach, and not, when I came to die, discover that I had not lived."—Henry Thoreau

"Often do the spirits of great events stride on before the events, and in today already walks tomorrow."—Samuel Taylor Coleridge

"To live in hearts we leave behind is not to die."—Thomas Campbell

"I have made this letter longer because I lack the time to make it shorter."—Blaise Pascal, illustrating the point that a well-composed letter requires time.

"War is cruelty. There is no use trying to reform it. The crueler it is, the sooner it will be over."—Civil War General William Tecumseh Sherman, stating his views on war from which the phrase "war is hell" was subsequently attributed to him.

"You find out life's this game of inches, and so is football. Because in either game, life or football, the margin for error is so small. I mean, one half a step too late or too early, and you don't quite make it."—Al Pacino, as his character head coach Tony D'Amato, talking to his football team before they took the field. (From the movie *Any Given Sunday*).

"In the factory we make cosmetics; in the store we sell hope."—Charles Revson

"An invasion of armies can be resisted, but not an idea whose time has come."—Victor Hugo

"Plain women know more about men than beautiful women do."—Katherine Hepburn

"As a human being, one has been endowed with just enough intelligence to be able to see clearly how utterly inadequate that intelligence is when confronted by what exists."—Albert Einstein

"Science cannot answer the deepest questions. As soon as you ask why there is something instead of nothing, you have gone beyond science. I find it quite improbable that such order came out of chaos. There has to be some organizing principle. God to me is the explanation for the miracle of existence—why there is something instead of nothing."—Cosmologist Allan R. Savage

"Your friend is the man who knows all about you, and still likes you."—Elbert Hubbard

"The woods are lovely, dark and deep. But I have promises to keep. And miles to go before I sleep. And miles to go before I sleep."—Robert Frost, from his poem *Stopping by Woods on a Snowy Evening*.

"Figuring out who you are is the whole point of human experience."—Anna Quindlen

"So let me assert my firm belief that the only thing we have to fear is fear itself—nameless, unreasoning, unjustified terror, which paralyzes needed efforts to convert retreat into advance."—President Franklin D. Roosevelt, said in the darkest days of the Great Depression.

"As every combat veteran knows, war is primarily sheer boredom punctuated by moments of stark terror."—Colonel Harry Summers

"Democracy is two wolves and a lamb deciding what to have for lunch."—Benjamin Franklin

"It is vain to be done with more what can be done with fewer."—William of Occam (1349). This principle became known as "Occam's Razor", which states that in attempting to explain some problem or event it is the simplest explanation that is probably the most accurate.

"It is not the strongest of the species that survive, nor the most intelligent, but the one most responsive to change."—Charles Darwin

"Children are the living messages we send to a time we will not see."—John H. Whitehead

"Luck is what happens when preparation meets opportunity."—Seneca

"You can make more friends in a month by being interested in them than in ten years by trying to get them interested in you."—Charles L. Allen

"Most problems precisely defined are already partially solved."—Harry Lorayne

"What have you done today to help reach your lifelong goals?"—Brian Tracy

"Decision is a sharp knife that cuts clean and straight. Indecision is a dull one that hacks and tears and leaves jagged edges behind."—Jan McKeithen

"ARBEIT MACHT FREI" (Work sets you free)—Infamous sign over the entrance to the largest extermination camp for Jews, in Auschwitz, Poland, during World War II. Ash flakes from the large, tall chimneys of the crematoriums, continually fell from the sky onto the camp 24 hours around the clock.

"Cause change and lead; accept change and survive; resist change and die."—Ray Norda

"The most important thing in communication is to hear what isn't being said."—Peter Drucker.

"If there is one single secret to long life, that secret is moderation."—George Gallup

"Everyone has an invisible sign hanging from their neck saying, 'Make me feel important'. Never forget this message when working with people."—Mary Kay Ash

"We do not quite forgive a giver. The hand that feeds us is in some danger of being bitten."—Ralph Waldo Emerson

"Sex is hardly ever just about sex."—Shirley McClaine

"There is only one boss: the customer. And he can fire everybody in the company, from the chairman on down, simply by spending his money someplace else."—Sam Walton, founder of Walmart.

"You shall not press down upon the brow of labor this crown of thorns, you shall not crucify mankind upon a cross of gold."—William Jennings Bryan, famed orator and 1896 presidential candidate, in the concluding words of his historic "Cross of Gold" acceptance speech to the Democratic convention, railing against the backing of U. S. currency by gold, which many saw as restricting the country's money supply resulting in the economic depression of the time. Immediately after uttering the above words, Bryan stepped back and threw his arms out to his sides in a Christ-like pose. After a few seconds of silence the convention audience exploded into a tumultuous roar that went on for several minutes.

"This is no time for making new enemies."—Voltaire, on his deathbed, on being asked to renounce the devil.

"Anyone who does not regularly gaze up and see the wonder and glory of a dark night filled with countless stars loses a sense of their fundamental connectedness to the universe."—Brian Greene

"Work expands to fill the time available for its completion."—Parkinson's Law

"I have a dream that my four little children will one day live in a nation where they will not be judged by the color of their skin, but by the content of their character."—Martin Luther King, Jr.

"No problem can withstand the assault of sustained thinking."—Voltaire

"I can feel guilty about the past, apprehensive about the future, but only in the present can I act. The ability to be in the present moment is a major component of mental wellness."—Abraham Maslow

"The pessimist complains about the wind; the optimist expects it to change; the realist adjusts the sails."—William Arthur Ward

"Don't sell the steak; sell the sizzle."—Elmer Wheeler

"There are three kinds of people; those that make things happen, those that watch things happen and those who don't know what's happening."—American proverb

"Efficiency is doing things right; effectiveness is doing the right things."—Peter Drucker

"Go confidently in the direction of your dreams. Live the life you have imagined."—Henry David Thoreau

"If I had eight hours to chop down a tree, I'd spend six hours sharpening my ax."—Abraham Lincoln

"There is hardly anything in the world that some man cannot make a little worse and sell a little cheaper, and the people who consider price only are this man's lawful prey."—John Ruskin. This quotation was engraved on a sign in the outer office of Dore Shary, head of production of Metro-Goldwyn-Mayer in the early 1950s.

"If you're alive, there's a purpose for your life. You were made by God and for God, and until you understand that, life will never make sense."—Rick Warren, church founder and author of "A Purpose Driven Life".

"Too often we underestimate the power of a touch, a smile, a kind word, a listening ear, an honest compliment, or the smallest act of caring, all of which have the potential to turn a life around."—Leo Buscaglia

"There are two things people want more than sex and money... recognition and praise."—Mary Kay Ash

"The trouble with not having a goal is that you can spend your life running up and down the field and never scoring."—Bill Copeland

"In playing ball, and in life, a person occasionally gets the opportunity to do something great. When that time comes, only two things matter: being prepared to seize the moment and having the courage to take your best swing."—Hank Aaron

"If you like laws and sausage, you should never watch either being made."—Otto von Bismarck

"Sometimes doing your best isn't good enough. Sometimes you need to do what is required."—Winston Churchill

"If I am to speak for ten minutes, I need a week for preparation; if fifteen minutes, three days; if half an hour, two days; if an hour, I am ready now."—Woodrow Wilson

"Markets can remain irrational far longer than you or I can remain solvent."—British economist John Maynard Keynes, commenting on the fact that although individual investors may be correct in their evaluation of a market security or condition, they cannot overcome the irrational mass action of other participants in the market.

"If you are not prepared to use force to defend civilization, then be prepared to accept barbarism."—Thomas Sowell

"Achievement seems to be connected with action. Successful men and women keep moving. They make mistakes, but they don't quit."—Conrad Hilton

"O God, give us serenity to accept what cannot be changed, courage to change what should be changed, and wisdom to distinguish the one from the other."—Reinhard Niebur (The Serenity Prayer)

"The buck stops here."—Famous sign on President Harry Truman's desk

"We don't receive wisdom; we must discover it for ourselves after a journey that no one can take for us or spare us."—Marcel Proust

"Remember that a man's name is to him the sweetest and most important sound in the language."—Dale Carnegie, author of *How to Win Friends and Influence People.*

"Don't make the mistake of letting yesterday use up too much of today."—Will Rogers

"Speak when you are angry and you will make the best speech you will ever regret."—Ambrose Bierce

"Be the change you wish to see in the world."—Mahatma Gandhi

"Continuous effort, not strength or intelligence, is the key to unlocking your potential."—Winston Churchill

"The only thing necessary for the triumph of evil is for good men to do nothing."—Edmund Burke

"The best way to predict your future is to create it."—Peter Drucker

"Do you want to know who you are? Don't ask. Act! Action will delineate and define you."—Thomas Jefferson

"Here is a test to find whether your mission on earth is finished: If you're alive, it isn't."—Richard D. Bach

"Remember that what you possess in this world will be found on the day of your death to belong to somebody else. But what you are will be yours forever."—Henry Van Dyke

"It was a question of saving hundreds of thousands of American lives. I couldn't worry what history would say about my personal morality. I made the only decision I knew how to make. I did what I thought was right."—Former President Harry S. Truman, commenting on his decision to drop the atomic bombs on Japan.

"The two highest achievements of the human mind are the twin concepts of loyalty and duty. Whenever these twin concepts fall into disrepute—get out of there fast! You may possibly save yourself but it is too late to save that society. It is doomed!"—Robert A. Heinlein

"The seductive promise of security from cradle to the grave is the real enemy of civilized society."—Alexis de Tocqueville

"In a hierarchy every employee tends to rise to his level of incompetence."—Laurence Peter, author of the "The Peter Principle".

"The unexamined life is not worth living."—Socrates

"The best argument against democracy is a five minute conversation with the average voter."—Winston Churchill

"The inarticulate speak longest."—Japanese Proverb

"It is not from the benevolence of the butcher, the brewer, or the baker, that we expect our dinner, but from their regard to their own self interest."—Adam Smith, eighteenth century economist, and author of *The Wealth of Nations*, who theorized that an "invisible hand" underpinned the actions of participants in a market economy.

"Compared to war, all other forms of human endeavor shrink to insignificance."—General George Patton

"You teach yourselves the law, but I train your minds. You come in here with a skull full of mush; you leave thinking like a lawyer."—Professor Kingsfield (John Houseman) from the movie *The Paper Chase*.

"I never worry about action, but only inaction."—Winston Churchill

"Those who can make you believe absurdities can make you commit atrocities."—Voltaire (72 virgins, anyone?)

"Nothing in the world can take the place of persistence. Talent will not; nothing is more common than unsuccesful men of talent. Genius will not; unrewarded genius is almost a proverb. Education will not; the world is full of educated derelicts. Persistence and determination alone are omnipotent."—President Calvin Coolidge

"Do not let what you cannot do interfere with what you can do."—John Wooden

"Planning for the future without a sense of the past is like planting cut flowers."—Daniel Boorstin, Pulitzer Prize winning historian

"No man has a memory long enough to be a successful liar."—Abraham Lincoln

"The individual's self-concept is the core of his personality. It affects every aspect of human behavior--the ability to learn, the capacity to grow and change. A strong, positive self-image is the best possible preparation for success in life."—Dr. Joyce Brothers

"Character is doing what's right when nobody is looking."—Congressional Representative J. C. Watts, Jr.

"We cannot change the cards we are dealt, just how we play the hand."—Randy Pausch, from "The Last Lecture".

"No one can make you feel inferior without your consent."—Eleanor Roosevelt

"I am the captain of my soul. I am the master of my fate."—William Henley, from his poem *Invictus*.

"Inaction breeds doubt and fear. Action breeds confidence and courage. If you want to conquer fear, do not sit home and think about it. Go out and get busy."—Dale Carnegie

"If I have lost confidence in myself, I have the Universe against me."— Ralph Waldo Emerson

"I'm a little wounded, but I am not slain/I will lay me down to bleed a while/Then I'll rise and fight again."—John Dryden

"You have enemies? Good. That means you've stood up for something, sometime in your life."—Winston Churchill

"Followers who tell the truth and leaders who listen are an unbeatable combination."—Warren Bennis

"Admonish your friends privately, but praise them publicly."—Publius Syrus

"In the fields of observation, chance favors only the prepared mind."— Louis Pasteur

"The leaders who offer blood, toil, tears and sweat always get more out of their followers than those who offer safety and a good time."— George Orwell

"The bitterest tears shed over graves are for words left unsaid and deeds left undone."—Harriet Beecher Stowe

"Unless you walk out into the unknown, the odds of making a profound difference in your life are pretty low."— Tom Peters

"Apply yourself. Get all the education you can, but then, by God, do something. Don't just stand there, make something happen."—Lee Iacocca

"I can't believe God put us on this earth to be ordinary."—Lou Holtz

"Carpe diem." ("Seize the day." i.e. act now)—Horace

"I never in my life learned anything from a man who agreed with me."—Dudley Malone

For those who are interested here is another group of outstanding quotations that didn't make the top list . . .

"Facts are stubborn things; and whatever may be our wishes, our inclinations, or the dictates of our passions, they cannot alter the state of facts and evidence."—John Adams, in defense of the British soldiers in the Boston Massacre trial.

"Let me not mourn for the men who died fighting, but rather let me be glad that such heroes have lived."—General George Patton

"We therefore commit his body to the ground; earth to earth, ashes to ashes, dust to dust."—Book of Common Prayer

"By recording your dreams and goals on paper, you set in motion the process of becoming the person you most want to be."—Mark Victor Hansen

"Under the Einstein formula ($E=mc^2$) a single gram of matter, four-tenths the weight of a dime, would lift a million-ton load to the crest of a mountain six miles high."—William Manchester, from his book *The Power and the Glory*.

"Rest is not idleness, and to lie sometimes on the grass on a summer day listening to the murmur of water, or watching the clouds float across the sky, is hardly a waste of time."—John Lubbock. And if we can't enjoy these moments in life, what's the point of living.

"We take the last carton of milk at the 7-11, unaware that we cause the guy behind us to drive four miles to the supermarket, where he runs into his long-lost girlfriend; they marry and have a child who grows up to discover a cure for cancer. Every day, each of us does things that move the lives of others—provoking thoughts, tipping decisions—in ways we know nothing about."—Andrew Stark, in a *Wall Street Journal* book review of *The Soul Hypothesis* by Mark C. Baker and Stewart Goetz

"No nation occupies a foot of land that was not stolen."—Mark Twain

"You've never lived until you've almost died. For those who fight for it, life has a meaning the protected will never know."—Leigh Wade

"Talent alone won't make you a success. Neither will being in the right place at the right time, unless you are ready. The most important question is: 'Are you ready?'"—Johnny Carson

"If you bungle raising your children nothing else much matters in life."—Jackie Kennedy

"This is all you have. This is not a dry run. This is your life. If you want to fritter it away with your fears, then you will fritter it away, but you won't get it back later."—Laura Schlessinger

"Abstract Art: A product of the untalented, sold by the unprincipled to the utterly bewildered."—Albert Camus

"When you're with someone who is dying, try to get in bed and snuggle with them. Often they feel very alone and just want to be touched. Many times my patients will tell me, 'I'm living with cancer but dying from lack of affection.'"—Registered nurse Barbara Dehn

"The big difference between sex for money and sex for free is that sex for money usually costs a lot less."—Brendan Behan

"I'm not about to raise two boys to be men by making them believe they are entitled to something just because they tried their best."—Pittsburgh Steelers linebacker James Harrison, after returning "participation" trophies of his two sons.

"A good teacher must know the rules; a good pupil, the exceptions."—Martin H. Fischer

"Under pressure you don't rise to the occasion, you sink to the level of your training."—A tenet of Navy Seal training

"To be truly feminine means being soft, receptive and submissive."—Gabrielle Reece, model and former professional volleyball player, standing 6 foot, 3 inches, commenting on her marriage to surfer Laird Hamilton, in her book, *My Foot Is Too Big For The Glass Slipper: A Guide To The Less Than Perfect Life.* This sentiment was immediately attacked by many social media commentators, saying she had set back the women's movement.

"As Americans we must always remember we all have a common enemy, an enemy who is dangerous, powerful and relentless. I refer, of course, to the federal government."— Dave Barry. Marquette University demanded that one of its graduate students remove this quotation, which had been posted on the student's door.

"The more you sweat in peace, the less you bleed in war."—Military maxim underlying the emphasis on keeping your forces highly trained at all times.

"War has a way of distinguishing between the things that are important and those that aren't"—Dialogue from the British Masterpiece Theater TV series *Downton Abbey*.

"I expect to die in bed, my successor will die in prison and his successor will die a martyr in the public square."—Cardinal Francis George, Archbishop of Chicago, commenting on the growth of the federal government and its intrusion into religious areas.

"Tomorrow, in a very real sense, your life—the life you author from scratch on your own—begins. . . I will hazard a prediction. When you are 80 years old, and in a quiet moment of reflection narrating for only yourself the most personal version of your life story, the telling that will be most compact and meaningful will be the series of choices you have made. In the end, we are our choices. Build yourself a great story."—Jeff Bezos, Amazon.com CEO, from a commencement address at Princeton University, May 30, 2010.

"You're tripping over dollars to find pennies."—Unknown. Used in the context that in the quest to find expense savings in a company's operations, many overlook the big picture with the potential of making significant savings, and instead focus on areas that will result in insignificant reductions in expenses.

"Demagoguery is the last refuge of the spineless politician willing to do anything to win the next election."— Florida Senator Marco Rubio, castigating his fellow senators, who were prepared to spend millions to attack those proposing changes to the unaffordable entitlement pro-grams that were driving the United States deeper and deeper into debt. From an article titled "Why I Won't Vote To Raise The Debt Limit" in *The Wall Street Journal.*

"The boss's job is not to evaluate. The boss's job is to make everyone a five."—Samuel Colbert, professor at UCLA's Anderson's School of Management, a dissenting voice to a widely used employee rank evaluation tool, "stacking", also derogatorily known as "rank and yank", promulgated by former General Electric CEO, Jack Welch. Under the stacking concept all of the employees in a defined group are ranked on a bell curve, with 10% being forced into a "1" ranking and destined to be separated from the company. Many companies are now moving away from the stacking concept deeming it artificial and not conducive to the development of a team concept. From an article by Shira Ovide in *The Wall Street Journal*.

"Lord save us from off-handed, flabby-cheeked, brittle-boned, weak-kneed, thin-skinned, pliable, plastic, spineless, effeminate, sissified three-carat Christianity."—Evangelist Billy Sunday

"What you're seeing is how a civilization commits suicide."—Camille Paglia, decrying the current trends in American society that, among others, devalue the military, undervalues manual labor and neuters male students. With regard to the last point she says, "They're making a toxic environment for boys. Primary education does everything it can to turn boys into neuters."

"What you are, I was, what I am, you will be."—Inscription (in Italian) on a banner held by sculpted skeletons over a doorway to a medieval church in Italy.

"The revolution devours its own."—Unknown. Based on an observation that some revolutions tend to become more radical as they age and the more radical elements turn on the original founders of a revolutionary movement, deeming them not sufficiently revolutionary. The French and Russian revolutions are outstanding examples of this observation.

"The best place to start looking when we are having problems in dealing with others is the last place we look—the mirror."—Unknown

"Despite what your Momma told you . . . violence does solve problems."— Quote inscribed around a skull shaped logo on merchandise manufactured by Craft International LLC apparel, a business founded by Chris Kyle, the American sniper credited with over 150 kills in Iraq.

"Surround yourself with the best people you can find, delegate authority, and don't interfere."— President Ronald Reagan, describing his philosophy regarding his staff and cabinet.

"The more arguments you win, the fewer friends you will have."— American proverb

"Whatever you think it's gonna take, double it. That applies to money, time, stress. It's gonna be harder than you think and take longer than you think."—Richard Cortese, on starting your own business. These words are just as applicable to any large project.

"Never be bullied into silence. Never allow yourself to be made a victim. Accept no one's definition of your life; define yourself."—Harvey Feirstein

"If you have an important point to make, don't try to be subtle or clever. Use a pile driver. Hit the point once. Then come back and hit it again. Then hit it a third time a tremendous whack."—Winston Churchill

"I don't want to get to the end of my life and find that I lived just the length of it. I want to have lived the width of it as well."—Diane Ackerman

"Probably the most honest 'self-made' man ever was the one we heard say, 'I got to the top the hard way—fighting my own laziness and ignorance every step of the way'."—James Thom

"When you're up against a tough problem, never quit. There's always one more thing you can do to influence any situation in your favor. And then after that, one more thing again. Never give up."—Retired Lt. Gen. Hal Moore, 40 years after leading his battalion to victory during a savage battle in the Ia Drang Valley in Vietnam, where he was outnumbered 4 to 1.

"KEEP CALM AND CARRY ON"—Words in a large framed sign on the wall behind the desk of Charlotte Steill, owner of Simply Put Organizing. The origin of this phrase dates back to England during World War II.

"**Dream what you want to dream—go where you want to go—try to be who you really are—because life is short and often gives us only a few chances to do the things that matter.**"—**Unknown**

"**Life is the ticket to the greatest show on earth.**"—**Unknown**

"**Live, so you do not have to look back and say: God, how I have wasted my life.**"-**Elizabeth Kubler-Ross**

"A frightened captain makes a frightened crew."—Lester Sinclair

"Power corrupts, and absolute power corrupts absolutely."—Lord Acton

"Candy is dandy, but liquor is quicker."—Ogden Nash

"Oh, what a tangled web we weave when first we practice to deceive."—Sir Walter Scott

"Let there be spaces in your togetherness."—Kahil Gibran

"Lead, follow, or get out of the way."—Unknown

"Sic semper tyrannus!" (Thus always to tyrants)—Actor John Wilkes Booth, words shouted to the audience after jumping to the stage from the theater box where he had assassinated President Lincoln.

"I saw an angel in the block of marble and I chiseled until I set him free."—Michelangelo

"All active mass movements strive to interpose a fact-proof screen between the faithful and the realities of the world. They do this by claiming that the ultimate and absolute truth is already embodied in their doctrine and that there is no truth nor certitude outside it. To rely on the evidence of the senses and reason is heresy and treason."—Eric Hoffer from his book *"The True Believer"*

"You are remembered for the rules you break."—General Douglas MacArthur

"I like not only to be loved, but to be told I am loved; the realm of silence is large enough beyond the grave."—George Eliot

"Liberté! Égalité! Fraternité! (Liberty! Equality! Fraternity!)—motto of the French Revolution

"If I stop one heart from breaking, I shall not live in vain."—Emily Dickinson, from her poem *Not In Vain.*

"Be sincere. Be brief. Be seated."—Franklin D. Roosevelt, giving advice on speechmaking.

"The creation of a thousand forests is in one acorn."—Ralph Waldo Emerson

"Sometimes the best, and only effective, way to kill an idea is to put it into practice."—Sydney J. Harris

"You don't have to be old in America to say of a world you lived in: That world is gone."—Peggy Noonan

"No man is an island, entire of itself;...any man's death diminishes me, because I am involved in mankind, and therefore never send to know for whom the bell tolls; it tolls for thee."—John Donne

"Show me the manner in which a nation or a community cares for its dead. I will measure exactly the sympathies of its people, their respect for the laws of the land, and their loyalty to high ideals."—William E. Gladstone

"In Italy for thirty years under the Borgias they had warfare, terror, murder, bloodshed—they produced Michelangelo, Leonardo da Vinci and the Renaissance. In Switzerland they had brotherly love, five hundred years of democracy and peace and what did that produce. . . ? The cuckoo clock." —Orson Welles's character, Harry Lime, from the movie *The Third Man*.

"I quote others only in order to better express myself."—Michel de Montaigne

"I love you, not only for what you are, but for what I am when I am with you."—Roy Croft

"Keep your fears to yourself; share your courage with others."—Robert Louis Stevenson

"A man never discloses his own character so clearly as when he describes another's."—Jean Paul Richter

"In peace, sons bury their fathers. In war, fathers bury their sons."—Herodotus

"Feeling sorry for yourself, and your present condition, is not only a waste of energy but the worst habit you could possibly have."—Dale Carnegie

"When the going gets tough, the tough get going."—Unknown. Motto seen printed, in large letters, on the barracks wall of the Heavy Weapons Platoon of Company B, 1st Airborne Battle Group, 503rd Infantry, 82nd Airborne Division, Fort Bragg, North Carolina, in February 1959.

"Keep in mind that the true meaning of an individual is how he treats a person who can do him absolutely no good."—Ann Landers

"In a place where there are no men, strive to be a man."—Yiddish proverb, where "man" translates as a "worthy human being."

"I fear not the man who has practiced 10,000 kicks once, but I fear the man who has practiced one kick 10,000 times."—Bruce Lee

"Hope is not a strategy. Luck is not a factor. Fear is not an option."—James Cameron. This quote was on the shirts given to the staff members working on the motion picture *Avatar*.

"As to methods, there may be a million, and then some, but principles are few. The man who grasps principles can successfully select his own methods."—Ralph Waldo Emerson

"As democracy is perfected, the office of the President represents, more and more closely, the inner soul of the people. On some great and glorious day, the plain folks of the land will reach their heart's desire at last and the White House will be occupied by a downright fool and complete narcissistic moron."—H. L. Mencken. The question is: Have we finally arrived at that point in the 21st century?

"We have no eternal allies, and we have no perpetual enemies. Our interests are eternal and perpetual, and those interests are our duty to follow."—Lord Palmerston (1848) expressing the paramount principle of foreign policy, followed by the leaders of all countries, past and present.

"War is God's way of teaching us geography."—Unknown

"It is better to suffer pain than to live in a world in which you don't allow yourself to be close enough to anybody to have the experience that's bound to give you suffering. And 'love guarantees suffering.'"—Eugene Kennedy, Professor Emeritus at Loyola University

"Joy and sorrow are inseparable. Together they come, and when one sits alone with you, remember that the other is nearby on your bed."— Kahil Gabron

"The best way to predict your future is to create it."—Peter Drucker

"If you risk nothing, then you risk everything."—Geena Davis

"Remember, gentlemen, an order that can be misunderstood will be misunderstood." —General von Moltke, Prussian general

"Your future depends on many things, but mostly on you."—Frank Tyger

"The hardest thing to learn in life is which bridge to cross and which to burn."—David Russell

"First-rate men hire first-rate men. Second-rate men hire third-rate men."—Leo Rosten

"Do not be arrogant because of your knowledge."—From the hieroglyphic writings of the Egyptian Ptahhope (2400 BC). Some personal guidance quotes are timeless.

Interested in more outstanding and thought-provoking quotes?

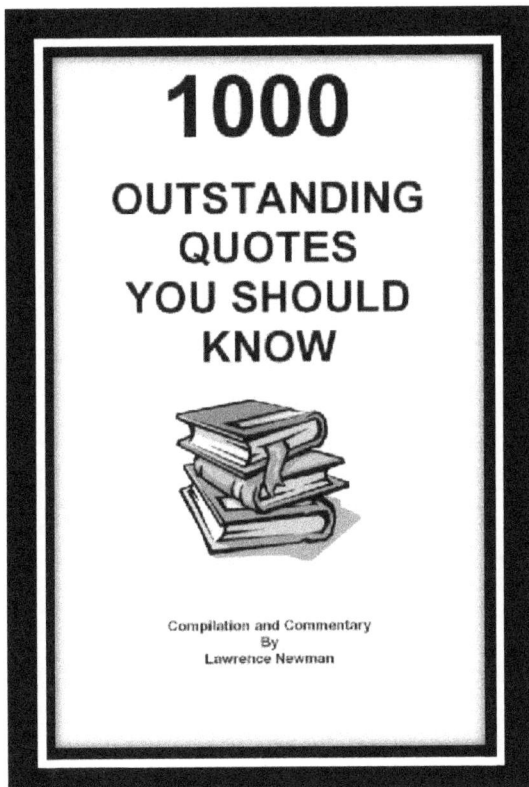

1000

OUTSTANDING
QUOTES
YOU SHOULD
KNOW

Compilation and Commentary
By
Lawrence Newman

Available on Amazon and Barnes and Noble internet book sites.